Recognizing Blessings in Disguise

*Spiritual Guidance for the
Covid-19 Pandemic*

Yogi Shanti Desai and
Edward Glazier, PhD

Special thanks to Gudjon Bergmann for typesetting and designing the cover. Gudjon is an accomplished thinker and author, whose 25+ books draw extensively on his own spiritual journey. He is a long-time friend and student of Yogi Shanti Desai.

Table of Contents

INTRODUCTION

Disaster and suffering are regular parts of human life in Maya (cosmic illusion). The world is presently facing disaster and suffering in the form of a pandemic. Many pandemics have occurred in the past. The present illness is an easily spread viral disease that impacts the respiratory and immune systems of people around the planet. The situation is challenging to society because it will persist for a prolonged period of time, because the cure requires people to behave in ways they are not used to, and because it is by definition a worldwide problem.

Physical distancing and hygiene, use of masks, development of medicines and vaccines, and time itself will eventually diminish the new coronavirus (COVID-19). Meanwhile, the pandemic is changing everyone's daily lives. It continues to cause physical suffering and death, financial hardship, and major challenges to government and to the medical and education systems. It has disrupted social life for all.

We have the choice in life to behave in ways that are beneficial to all. The simple disciplines of wearing a mask and giving distance prevent illness for both self and others. But many people do not understand that we are all connected. Many are selfish or deluded and unwilling to alter their behaviors. The situation has created stress and anxiety for the masses. It has angered many people and they blame others. Some hold anger inside and suffer from worries, fear, and depression. People are used to the lifestyle and freedom of going to social events, restaurants, and family gatherings. Although people know that regulating their activities can save lives, they feel locked down and suffocated. Many become stir crazy. Some become habituated to computer devices and constant information, politics, shallow religious beliefs, divisive ideologies. Some lose hope and become dependent on alcohol and other substances.

Some people are less affected by the pandemic. Those with wisdom recognize the temporary nature of the situation and see opportunity for individual and collective growth. Wise people already practice some disciplines and regulate their own behavior. They appreciate and are thankful what they have. They make selfless sacrifices for others.

True spiritual seekers continually recognize the impermanence of life. They recognize that the body and mind are merely changing reflections of Atman (soul). They feel the connection of all things through Supreme Consciousness. What seem like disciplines to others are natural ways of living to the seeker. Life flows, and the seeker flows with changes, like winter into spring and spring into summer. The pandemic is considered an opportunity to use time wisely, to go within with less distraction, to appreciate the simple pleasures of connecting with nature. "Disaster" is seen as a natural event or time of change, like the covering of a seed that is destroyed so the flower can bloom.

If one gets glimpses of the simplified ancient philosophy discussed in this short book, they will find hope and encouragement to restart life with enthusiasm. This will give one vision to turn calamities into gifts and curses into blessings. It will awaken you from self-created illusions and will provide the direction needed to find bliss in spite of turmoil in the world. This is an ideal time in history to wake up and embrace or renew the path to Self and truth. Knock and the doors shall open. Ask and ye shall receive. Personal guidance on the path is available from Yogi Shanti Desai. It is at your convenience through the internet. Be humble and make contact.

RECOGNIZING THE BENEFITS

A Surplus of Time

The pandemic is changing the way humans inter-act. Routine schedules are disrupted. In reality, there is now more time for self and family. Now is the time to explore Self or God within. But the human mind has the tendency to procrastinate and wait for ideal conditions in the future or to wait for retirement when other aspects of life are finished. But the time is always now. Retirement may never come. One has to see opportunity in the present moment. Lockdowns and restrictions confine you at home and that gives you opportunity to utilize time properly. Time enables one to accomplish important tasks. Time can also be seen an important commodity. Time is money. But neither time nor money bring happiness of themselves. One needs to prioritize one's goal in life and bring time and money into achieving the goal. The real goal of life is to know the permanent Self within and attain bliss.

- People become workaholics and forget that time and money are best used to achieve health and happiness of body and mind.
- Time allows you to catch up with all the tasks you were postponing.
- It allows you to settle down and think clearly.
- You get the chance to evaluate your life and practice introspection.
- You can get joy from simple activities in life when you have time.
- Enjoyment does not come from more toys or electronic gadgets but rather when you have the time and stillness of mind to relax. You can enjoy just sitting, looking at the sky, trees, or waves of the ocean.
- You can spend more time with family members and improve communication.
- You can dedicate time to your hobbies.
- One gets the chance to read and contemplate.
- Use this unique opportunity to cultivate these family activities: family prayer, sitting for a meal with no electronics, breathing and meditating together.

A Chance for Serenity

During times of stress and calamity, one naturally calls on God for assistance. But we should realize that we are co-creators of our destiny. We can change some things but not others. We can care for self and others wholeheartedly during the pandemic, but we cannot stop the disease ourselves. We are an important part of the whole, but we must accept that we can do only so much in our own way. This knowledge brings serenity of mind.

"God, grant me the serenity to accept the things I cannot change; courage to change things I can; and wisdom to know the difference"

Theologian Reinhold Niebur (1892-1971)

The Serenity to Accept

- Acceptance is looking in the mirror to face our self.
- Acceptance removes illusions and allows one to face reality.
- Accept and love yourself as you are.
- You are the center of the universe and the starting point of the universe.
- Acceptance allows you to recognize the starting point for exploring and utilizing your hidden potential.

Serenity comes from accepting things by surrendering to the Supreme. Surrendering means attunement. We merge our will to the will of the Supreme, become an instrument, and remain peaceful. We learn to surrender and become free from imaginary burdens. We have little control over what is happening around us. Supreme Lord creates, manages, and transforms everything. We learn to accept this reality. We become grateful for all the gifts of God and see opportunity for coming closer to God instead of complaining.

Maintaining Serenity during Large-Scale Cycles of Change (Yugas)

Scriptures discuss cosmic cycles of birth, sustainment of life, and death or destruction. One age leads to the next. Accept the cyclic changes. It is inevitable reality. When you comprehend this, you feel relief from all anxieties. You feel the presence of the supreme Lord within your heart that protects you at all times. You become free from illusions and imaginary burdens. Dissolve the ego (separate I-Consciousness) and merge with the Supreme Consciousness.

God is Supreme Consciousness that creates, sustains, and destroys. This is called the cycle of yuga. Everything in the universe follows this cycle. Day and night, the change of the seasons, and birth and death are the realities of life. Some insects have a short life span, while animals have a longer life span. Trees, mountains, oceans, and our sun have much longer life spans. The cycle repeats itself. Our planet also has beginning and end. The cycle repeats itself. According to many authorities and some scriptures, the universal cycle is made of four Yugas, much like morning, afternoon, evening, and night. Morning comes at the end of the night. We are currently at the end of the cycle called Kali yuga. Kali yuga means period of spiritual darkness. Immorality and exponential changes take place. Nature produces calamities and destruction for regeneration. There is no doomsday or eternal hell or heaven. The dualities of life and life cycles awaken us to evolve spiritually. We should accept Kali yuga as a blessing. It gives us the opportunity for quicker evolution and transformation.

Destruction means transformation. A seed breaks to become a tree. We can break free of our self-imposed limitations to flow in rhythm with the universe. But we cannot comprehend the divine plan with our limited mind. We carry an imaginary burden on our shoulders and suffer. We can surrender the mind and feel instant relief.

Accepting Change in the Material Universe

The entire external universe is constantly changing. It is impermanent. It is called Sansara. By accepting the changing nature of Sansara and the permanent nature of Self (Atman), we remain peaceful.

It is the blessing of the Supreme that things change constantly. Imagine if our body did not age or die and that things and situations did not change. The world would become stagnant and boring. Acceptance of constant change gives us joy as we wake up and start a new day. At death, the journey of the soul (Jivatma) continues in a new body with fresh enthusiasm.

Accept the duality of nature and the permanent nature of Self. Duality means two opposite forces. Pleasure and pain, gain and loss, honor and insult are integral parts of life. Negative makes us appreciate positive. Hunger produces appetite, tiredness produces sleep, heat of summer gives us appreciation of the winter, and vice versa. By maintaining equilibrium (Samata) and flowing with changes, including societal disasters, we can remain peaceful.

The Courage to Change Things We Can Change

As we grow more peaceful, knowledgeable, and energetic, we are able to make beneficial changes in our lives. In this way, we become naturally helpful to others and society. This is everyone's Dharma or duty.

- Dharma (duty) sustains the entire universe.
- Dharma is guided by intuitive wisdom.
- Dharma is the foundation of the spiritual journey.
- Dharma brings harmony and joy individually and collectively.

We need courage to change things by performing our Dharma. It is called Karma yoga. We perform our duty as suitable to our age, capabilities, profession, family, neighbors, nation, and nature. When we accept the reality of existence, we use our skills, knowledge, and energy to serve selflessly without attachment to results. This gives us peace and freedom.

When we act in accordance with Dharma, we begin to see the permanent nature of our consciousness which is the spark of God (Self) and always blissful. We learn to tune into Self and remain blissful during times of turmoil in the world.

We are put on the Earth to learn lessons by serving selflessly. The entire creation is involved in serving. The trees, rivers, sun, moon, and oceans serve unconditionally. Practicing Dharma brings peace and freedom in life.

Animals are peaceful because they follow instinct and the rhythm of nature. Human birth is the climax of evolution. We have intellect and consciousness. If we misuse the intellect and fail to act in our best interest, we can experience less peace than animals. If we use purified intellect, we can receive intuition and direction for Self-realization. We can experience lasting peace by renunciation of deep desires.

The Wisdom to Choose

Life presents us with many options and choices on a regular basis. Wisdom comes when our choices are based on deep intuition and purified intellect. In reality, it takes only a little reflection to realize that our choices affect both self and others. For instance, deep down everyone knows that wearing a mask and keeping a reasonable distance during a pandemic of respiratory disease protects self, family, and community.

- Purified intellect tunes into Supreme Consciousness which produces wisdom.
- Wisdom transcends all limitations of time and space.
- Intellect is purified by being still, introverted, and connecting with Atman or Soul.
- Wisdom gives panoramic vision to see reality as it is.
- Wisdom gives firsthand experience of the permanent Self behind the ever-changing world.
- Wisdom removes dualities of pleasure/pain, gain/loss, honor/insult.
- Wisdom liberates us.

When pure intellect tunes into Supreme Consciousness, we gain intuitive wisdom and this guides our life. Wisdom allows us to observe ourselves and the world. We can perceive the impermanent nature of life and the permanent nature of Self. This is called spiritual discernment (Vivek). It produces effortless renunciation. We are not tempted by worldly illusions. We dwell on the Self and ignore the impermanent world as a dream or illusion.

This book gives direction and guidance for gaining true wisdom. The guidance is based on time-tested ancient teachings of the masters. You can apply the principles to remain peaceful.

AN OPPORTUNITY TO WAKE UP

The pandemic is a wake-up call, reminding us to look for permanence within. This is true of all disasters and calamities in life. We become complacent and forget that life is temporary. We become satisfied with illusion until it shakes us awake. The wise remain awake at all times.

- To wake up means to become fully conscious, remove old conditions, illusions, and escapes, and to practice introspection.
- We can awaken when we contemplate who we really are, the true purpose of life, and the best direction in life.
- We can take the path of virtue with priority, urgency, intensity, and enthusiasm.
- When we become fully awakened, we gain enough energy to make a quantum leap to a new level of transformation.

We are currently going through a pandemic virus, which has disturbed the ways of life of human beings around the world. For many, this has furthered the tendency to become lazy and mechanical, to drag through life aimlessly. We can alter this tendency by waking up from our conditioning (Sanskaras), by using deep intuition and by thinking creatively. We can avoid repeating patterned behaviors life after life.

We wake up partially when we accomplish something meaningful or experience shocks that make us question what to do. But we often go back to patterns that keep us from experiencing who we really are (Atman). We can wake up permanently to bliss by being grateful for all things and facing shock as opportunities for deepening our understanding of Self or God.

The ongoing pandemic has created a deep and lasting shock to human societies and cultures around the globe. As individuals, spiritual awakening occurs when one uses the shock to wake up permanently and change direction in life. As more individuals awaken to Self, life on the planet will also change direction.

Human life is precious. It is the climax of evolution and should be utilized for Self-realization, instead of merely survival, pleasure, power, or laziness. We can use awareness to see the pandemic as a wake-up call. With awareness we can wake up, think clearly and experience the eternal reality. With awareness, we can turn curses into blessings. Without awareness, everything feels like curse. We regret, complain, and become miserable.

Guidance:

- Practice short meditation or pray first thing upon waking up.
- Read and contemplate on the affirmations given at the end of this book.
- Practice quantum leap meditation in the morning and before going to sleep.
- View your day and consciously choose activities that support your goal.
- During the day, take time to relax mind and body. Slow down and breathe for a few minutes.
- Feel your connection with inner Self and with nature. Wake up.
- Before bed, forgive others and yourself for mistakes made during the day.
- Clear the mind of sanskaras (conditioning and impressions).
- Contemplate your affirmations, relax, and fall asleep.

Mindfulness

The pandemic offers the opportunity to be mindful. Mindfulness requires becoming a passive observer. It involves maintaining a non-judgmental state of heightened awareness of thoughts, emotions, and experiences.

- It is the conscious direction of awareness toward the present moment.
- One gets opportunity to be mindful of all activities. One can slow down eating and walking.
- One saves energy by stopping judgment of people and experiences.
- One can observe instead of engaging the chattering mind.
- One slows down impulsive and compulsive activities.
- One learns to think before speaking or acting.
- One learns patience with self and others.
- Mindfulness prepares one for consistent awareness.

Heightened Awareness

Disasters and suffering bring awareness that the world is always changing. It is not reliable. The pandemic heightens our awareness that life in the world is fragile. It reminds us that our time in this body is limited. We are encouraged to look for peace and permanence within.

- Awareness means gaining vision to see what you could not see before.

- We are covered with darkness of ignorance. Awareness is the torch light to remove darkness.
- Awareness wakes us up from the cosmic illusion of Maya.
- Awareness teaches us lessons and converts curses into blessings.

Awareness is the product of consciousness. When pure intellect works with consciousness, it turns into mindfulness and awareness. During mindfulness one observes all perceptions without judgment. Mindfulness leads one into awareness. Awareness is the dynamic and creative form of flowing mindfulness. Awareness involves vigilance and alertness in observing, drawing inferences and conclusions from firsthand experience. With awareness one can use intuitive wisdom and sensitivity on a regular basis. This transforms life.

With awareness, one learns that Supreme Consciousness is eternal and uses the forces of nature (Prakriti) to create, sustain, and destroy. These forces follow the law of Karma and underlay the cycles of day/night, the seasons, and the creation and destruction of the physical world. It is called Leela or divine play of the Lord.

The cyclic changes help the soul (Jivatma) to learn lessons and evolve. Destruction in reality is transformation. Transformation allows evolution to take place.

Life in the world is like a long dream. Because of ignorance and conditioning, everything we experience looks real and we become attached to it. This is cosmic illusion (Maya). All creatures are born and die in front of our eyes yet we consider our physical selves to be immortal. With awareness we see the impermanent nature of the world and the permanent nature of consciousness (Self). We remain at the center and observe the changing world as a dream. Supreme Consciousness dwells within our heart. When we get connected to it, we become free.

Aloneness

Avoiding extensive contact with others in close proximity and wearing masks are easy ways to help diminish the pandemic. Being alone with self and nature on a regular basis allows one to prevent transmission and infection of the virus. Aloneness can be seen as a blessing. Peace occurs in proportion to a quiet mind, which is fostered by quiet meditation and the ability to be alone with joy.

Most people dislike aloneness. Wise people see the value of aloneness. Spiritual seekers enjoy aloneness.

- Aloneness means being attuned to Self and being content within the Self.

- One remains content without stimulation of senses or the mind.
- Aloneness is synonymous with being in the present, transcendence of the mind, the power of now, and inner stillness.
- Aloneness connects one to the inexhaustible source of bliss and intuitive wisdom.
- Aloneness connects you to the source of Consciousness, from which the universe is projected.
- Aloneness is not loneliness. One remains peaceful whether in seclusion or in the presence of others.
- Being alone stops the wastage of energy that can be utilized for intuitive wisdom and creative activities.
- One can make a direct quantum leap to the source within the spiritual heart (Atman).
- Aloneness is not loneliness. One remains peaceful in seclusion or noisy crowd.

We are programmed from childhood to seek happiness from outside. We work and spend our entire life in the search of happiness in the world. Our activities are motivated by the ideas of earning money, buying houses and cars, earning comforts, fame, power, and social status. We run in circles by not knowing the truth. We seek a social life. We shop, watch television, or listen to music to stimulate our senses and mind. When we do not find stimulation, we become bored and lonely. This is happening to many people deprived of their normal patterns of stimulation during the pandemic.

In reality, the permanent happiness of bliss is our basic nature. All external stimulation excites the senses and the mind only temporarily. This is followed by pain or dissatisfaction and a search for new stimulation. If we observe with awareness, we find that happiness actually occurs at the moment when desires are fulfilled and we become introverted. The feeling of pleasure actually comes in the moment as we briefly connect with our Source after winning a ball game, solving a puzzle, or reconnecting with a loved one, as examples. This brief connection with Self or Source is unlike longer or continual connection with Self that is achievable by quieting the mind. The nature of Self is bliss. Bliss is the continuous flow of happiness. It does not rely on external stimulation and does not diminish with time. In illusion, we think that happiness comes from outside and we continue search in the world instead of within.

Peace comes in proportion to introversion and suffering comes in proportion to extroversion. When we understand this mechanism, we stop running outward and learn to find peace within. We change to a lifestyle that promotes inner stillness and aloneness.

We are born alone and empty-handed. We leave alone and leave empty-handed. Everyone is in the same predicament. We cannot change this for anyone, nor can anyone change this for us.

We can serve others for our purification and evolution. No one can eat for us or take our pain away. Others can inspire us and guide us but we have to follow the lonely path. We start to evolve spiritually only when we take charge of our own life. True, lasting happiness comes by being alone with the Self. Being alone means withdrawing attention from the sense organs, motor organs, and the mind, and being content within the Self. This is called sense withdrawal (Pratyahara).

During the pandemic we find that the virus restricts our normal activities. Instead of complaining, we should accept this as an opportunity to begin to slow down and remove reliance on external stimulus and entertainment. In reality, it can take years to cultivate the stillness and silence needed to transcend mind and body at will. All the inspiration toward that end comes by being alone and cultivating connection with our own Self.

Pratyahara is the fifth step of Raja Yoga. One cuts down on activities of motor organs and sense organs along with the mind. By restraining these, one enters the stages of concentration, meditation, and Samadhi. Samadhi is full integration with Self.

One who is locked down due to the virus can use this time as a chance to restrain the senses and practice aloneness with Self for contemplation. One can use the time and situation as an opportunity to grow.

Guidance:

- Get in habit of sitting quietly twice a day with eyes closed and observe the breath passively.
- Focus deep within the heart. Experience shining light that spreads peace and love through your body and ultimately to the world.
- Practice observing silence and talk sparingly with conscious awareness.
- Practice restraining stimulation from sights and sounds.
- Practice mindfulness in walking, talking, eating, and chores to tame the mind.
- Practice quantum leap meditation regularly.

Direction in Life

Time alone allows us to contemplate. This is an excellent time in history to contemplate the nature of the world, our lives, and our reason for being here. We can ask ourselves "who am I?," "what am I doing with my life?," "where is my life going with the time I have left?" Sit quietly and observe the answers. In truth:

- We are separated from Supreme Consciousness.
- We are all learning lessons and are returning to the Source like a prodigal son.
- Everyone evolves toward Self at their own speed.
- Spiritual seekers can speed up the journey by making a quantum leap within.

Everyone is seeking permanent happiness and peace. Some seek in the material world while others seek in the spiritual world.

What we perceive is the reality. Eternal reality is always blissful and free. World reality is projected by the mind. Mind perceives the sensations from the senses, adds emotions and associates with past memories. This obscures the reality of Self within.

This is called Maya or cosmic illusion. It is like a long dream. Dream is real as long as we are dreaming. The purpose of life is to wake up from the cosmic dream and experience the essence of Self, which is eternal reality.

We are Jivatma (Soul), or Atman in bondage. We are separated from Paramatma (Supreme Consciousness) and will return back to Paramatma. Yogi Patanjali states that the world is given to Jivatma to enjoy and learn lessons. One can get lost in illusion and forget the goal of life.

The world looks attractive but it is like a prison. It produces restrictions and limitations of time and space. A prisoner becomes comfortable over time and forgets about freedom. A wise person senses freedom within and loses attraction to the world. The restrictions and disciplines needed to diminish the pandemic do not bother the wise person who already understands the blessings of time and freedom to look within.

Everyone evolves at their own speed and learns lessons, repeating them as necessary. The spiritual path is circular. Any step away from home (Self) is also the first step toward realizing that the world offers only illusion.

Jivatma's journey toward the world is an external journey. The spiritual journey is inward. One has to get rid of laziness (Tamas), become active (Rajas), and then find balance and peace (Satva). One has to succeed in the world to enable a straightforward spiritual journey. World is a school that prepares one for the college of the spiritual journey.

Material and Spiritual Success

The pandemic affords us time and solitude. These can be used profitably for achieving success in life. Real success incorporates all aspects of life.

- Disciplines for material and spiritual success are the same.
- One merely has to change direction from the world to the Atman.
- One who cannot succeed in the material life cannot succeed in spiritual life.
- All experiences of material life become helpful for spiritual success.

<u>Guidance:</u>

- *Clarify the primary goal.* One needs clarity of goal and the flexibility to change the means as necessary. One's primary goal in life should be Self-knowledge. This goal is not like material goals that are accompanied by anxiety regarding the results. This goal is taking the path of virtue (Dharma) and enjoying the freedom of flowing with life without anxiety. The spiritual path gives joy in the beginning, in the middle, and at the end. It survives death as one continues the journey of Jivatma (individual) back home to Paramatma (God) from life to life.

- *Utilize secondary goals.* Secondary goals are for managing material life that supports the spiritual journey. One needs surplus of health, time, money, and wisdom to support the spiritual journey. A lack of surplus produces hindrance. Secondary goals enable management of material life that best supports the spiritual journey.

1. *Health*: The body is the fundamental means for the material and spiritual journey. Body is the field that supports sense organs, motor organs, mind, and intellect. Atman (Soul) is the knower or witness of the field. One needs surplus energy in the body, senses, and the mind for success. One has a duty to self and others to take care of the body during the pandemic, taking appropriate steps to prevent viral infection or transmission, and to support one's own immune system. Body is like a ferry boat. It does not need pampering but must be maintained to make the journey.

2. *Money*: One needs a surplus of money to achieve the time, appropriate conditions, and freedom for undertaking spiritual activities without interruption. One may need creativity to identify new ways or earning money during the pandemic. One can also use the time to practice conservation of existing funds. Money is a means to an end—don't get lost in the process of earning it.

3. *Time*: In the modern era, time is a critical factor in daily life. One can manage money and time to create surplus

by simplifying life to suit changing situations. A shortage of time, money, or energy produces stress. Time and money can buy each other. They cannot buy health and wisdom.

4. *Wisdom*: Wisdom is the most important of all secondary goals. It can help one bypass all hardships. One can employ wisdom when money and time are limited, or during sickness and other challenges. A wise person knows that successes and failures are cyclic and maintains equanimity during both. Wisdom can function to balance life and provide direction during disaster and crisis. Wisdom gives one panoramic vision of life and the world. Wisdom recognizes impermanence and illusion. This keeps one awake on the path to Self. True wisdom is gained by being still and introverted and connecting with Supreme Consciousness. Wisdom can also be attained by mindfulness, living with conscious awareness, and practicing spiritual discernment (Vivek). One learns lessons from pleasant and unpleasant experiences. Spiritual discernment produces renunciation (Vairagya). One sees the impermanent nature of things and loses thirst for

pleasure effortlessly. One does not need any effort. The pandemic is a reminder of the impermanent and uncertain nature of external life.

- *Employ Synchronicity.* One can synchronize the subconscious mind with the conscious mind using affirmations. Subconscious mind provides emotional support. Synchronize thoughts and emotions. Use visualization and day-dreaming to support your goal.

- *Recognize the Power of Love.* The power of heart is many times more powerful that power of the mind. Infinite bliss and love are the ultimate goals.

- *Make Beneficial Decisions.* Take time before making decisions. Do not let the mind oscillate like a pendulum.

- *Commitment.* Stay committed. Take responsibility for your life. Give up dependence on others. Be willing to sacrifice comforts when necessary.

- *Accept Austerity (Tapas).* Follow the path with love and face problems such as the pandemic with a smile.

- *Avoid Procrastination.* Avoid lethargy, laziness, and postponement. Invent new, creative ways to engage yourself and keep your practice vibrant.

- *Set Priorities.* Prioritize your primary and secondary goals in life. Bring your daily activities in line with your goals and remember the ultimate goal.

- *Develop a Sense of Urgency.* Create a sense of urgency for achieving the goal. This helps one avoid procrastination. Life is short and uncertain. The pandemic makes this clear.

- *Use Intensity.* Add power to your intention and practices with intensity of focus.

- *Be Creative.* Think out of the box, cultivate intuition, and make a quantum leap toward your goal.

- *Practice Swadhyay.* Contemplate the teachings of the scriptures. Practice introspection and Self inquiry. Ask "Who am I?"

- *Seek out Satsang (Truth).* Maintain contact with inspirational friends and groups, and study inspirational scriptures. Seek out those who tell the truth.

- *Find Inspiration.* Get recharged by contemplating on the teachings of great masters and by practicing stillness, introspection, and meditation.

- *Maintain Enthusiasm.* Sustain enthusiasm by interacting with spiritual people, affirming your goal, and feeling the presence of infinite Self within.

- *Be Patient and Persevere.* Be committed to steady, rhythmic practice without becoming attached to the results. Know that all things will pass.

- *Use Affirmations.* Practice positive affirmations daily and before going to sleep.

- *Maintain and Undercurrent of Dedication to the Goal.* Continually sustain the undercurrent of your goal at all levels of your consciousness. A spiritual undercurrent guides our physical and mental activities.

- *Surrender.* After applying the above principles, just relax. Remove all burdens from mind. Surrender to Supreme Consciousness. Expand your consciousness. Tune into universal consciousness for guidance and support.

ADDITIONAL GUIDANCE

"Brahman is perfect. Jagat is perfect. Jagat is projected from Brahman. When Jagat is destroyed in time, Brahman still remains intact. Brahman is indivisible and remains as individual Atman with identical qualities of Brahman"

- Simplified essence of the Isavasya Upanishad.

Supreme Consciousness is Eternal

- Brahman (God or Universal Soul) is Eternal Consciousness. Brahman has no beginning, no end, and no boundaries. It includes and transcends all things, including physical health and sickness.
- The entire physical universe is born, continues for billions of years, and eventually dies within Supreme Consciousness.
- Brahman is untouchable, just like space is not touched by fire, flood, or disease.
- Brahman is indivisible.

- Brahman is the source of happiness and bliss.
- We are Supreme Consciousness but have forgotten because of the influence of Maya.

The Material Universe is Maya (Impermanent)

- The material universe (Jagat) changes constantly.
- All sentient and insentient beings are interconnected and permeated with consciousness and energy.
- Everything solid, liquid, or gas is nothing but the interplay of electromagnetic energy.
- The three forces of nature (Tamas, Rajas, and Satva) follow the law of Karma (cause and effect) and maintain the equilibrium of the universe.

The material universe functions through Brahman. It is illusive because it changes with time, space, and situations. Brahman underlies all things, like the sun that reflects in many containers. It vivifies the material universe. The sun remains intact when the containers are removed. Brahman is like a movie screen on which the physical universe is projected. The screen is not touched by the projection of the film. The film is invisible due to the darkness of ignorance, while the screen becomes visible with the light of knowledge.

Our life is relatively real as long as we are alive. Our experiences are real. But everything is temporary and changes constantly. We are engrossed with the experiences of life and identify ourselves with the body, senses, and mind and forget that we are Consciousness. In reality, we can consciously use body, senses, and mind, as instruments.

All suffering is the result of ignorance about our true nature (Avidya). Because of ignorance we carry burdens on our shoulders and get attached to impermanent objects, people, and ideologies. We become the victims of dualities and divisions such as you and I, and us and them. Division is the cause of suffering.

Supreme Reality and Relative Realities are Coexistent

If we maintain awareness of the Ultimate and limited realities simultaneously, we find joy in material life while evolving spiritually.

- If we dwell on Supreme Reality alone and ignore mundane life, we become escapists and remain in illusion.
- If we ignore Supreme Reality and accept material life as the only reality, we become victims of the world and our own desires. We will take the hurtful path and spread problems to others.

- If we accept relative reality and deal with it wholeheartedly while performing our Dharma, we can flow with life.
- If we surrender the fruits of our actions to the Supreme while maintaining awareness of Self as undercurrent, we can experience bliss.

Guidance:

1. Live Like a Traveler

Our stay in the world is brief. We are like travelers. Enjoy your short vacation by being in the present. Do not build attachments to things or people. Be compassionate to all beings. They are short-term acquaintances. Learn to endure hardships. These are only temporary.

2. Play Your Role Efficiently (Dharma)

Skillful action is called Karma yoga. It gives peace and liberates. Skillful action means selfless action and does not produce karma or sanskaras (lasting impressions). We are not the owners or enjoyers. Our limited minds and egos did not create the universe. Remove the burdens of ownership. We are only instruments of God. We use our body, senses, and mind to serve.

- Remove the illusion of doer-ship. Supreme Reality carries all human burdens.

- You do not carry your luggage while you fly on a plane or ride on a train.
- Remember "Thy will be done" and surrender your burdens.
- Play your role efficiently. This is our Dharma It gives us freedom and peace.
- Work selflessly without ego. You will not build Sanskaras. Your consciousness will expand.
- Accept the results of your action as blessings of God (Prasad).
- Remember that after playing this short role you will go home and rest.
- If you play the role of a sick old person for an hour, you remember in the background who you really are and that you will be your original self again at the end of the play.
- Always remember your permanent essence as you move through life.

3. Remain as an Observer (Drishta) or Witness (Sakshi)

Remain an observer and passive witness to ongoing changes in life without reacting to them. In actuality, you are unchanging subjective experience of Supreme Consciousness. Body, senses, mind, emotions and impressions are changing objects. You are Atman and have the qualities of eternal existence and conscious awareness of bliss in the background. You are the center of the universe. The world revolves around you. You are like the calm center of a wheel or hurricane. You rest peacefully at the center while all things are in orbit around you. You can remain as blissful consciousness untouched by fluctuating dualities and divisions of life.

4. Remain as a Humble Instrument and not the "Doer" (Karta)

Supreme Consciousness manages the universe using the law of Karma (cause and effect). In illusion we carry burdens that are not our own. We transcend identities as the actors (Karta), owners, or enjoyers (Bhokta). We can use our bodies, minds, and senses to serve selflessly and become instruments through which to experience bliss. Otherwise, we generate impressions in the subconscious mind (Sanskaras). These bind us to the cycle of transmigration. By being an instrument, a non-doer, we become free from the law of Karma even if we undertake activities in the world

5. Establish Friendship with the Mind

- Our mind can be our best friend or worst enemy.
- The unconscious mind retains sanskaras of past experiences, habits, and conditioning.
- Conditioning is more influential than will power.
- We can remove old conditioning by practicing mindfulness and conscious awareness.
- We can replace old sanskaras with new affirmations. We can remove deep sanskaras through meditation

- Mind is impulsive. Mind wants quick gratification and chooses an easy path which produces long term problems. Mind avoids the path of austerity which brings permanent freedom.
- Mind wants quick results. It has no patience. It changes paths if it does not get expected results.
- Mind can pretend to be a friend but sabotage us with reasons for not continuing or focusing wholeheartedly on the goal.
- Remember that we are not mind or body, but rather part of Supreme Consciousness.
- Because the Goal is infinitely rewarding, there is no reason to stop treading the path; in reality, the path to God is closest to your heart.
- Make friends with the mind and gently inquire within about the truth of our reasons for not starting or continuing on the path.

6. Excuses for Waiting and Reasons for Persisting

- "I cannot presently afford to spend time or resources on the path." [in reality, all activities and resources can at any moment be internally directed to the ultimate goal].
- "I don't have the time right now." [time is always running out, now is always the time to make some time].
- "I shall start tomorrow." [today is always the day to start the journey anew].
- "I will wait for the right time." [it is always the right time. Time, tide, and crisis wait for no

one, and the seeker can prepare for both crisis and happiness by always practicing awareness and love].

- "I am waiting for an invitation." [Other people are busy with their own lives and cannot be relied on; Self is always waiting and inviting the seeker to look within].
- "I need encouragement from someone." [inspiration can be attained through Satsang (discussion of Truth) and persistent practice; look to your inner self or spiritual guide for encouragement].
- "I know almost everything about yoga and spirituality." (there is no end to what can be known through wisdom and that which can be experienced in the heart).
- "I have studied with famous masters and have spent lots of money to earn my degree or certification" [the humble traveler knows that the real path is internal, must be tread alone, and that the results are not visible to others].
- "I have made so much progress that I do not need anyone's help [subtle pride and ego are major hindrances on the journey; these tend to fade during times of crisis]."
- "I feel guilty for not practicing or treading the path with sincerity in the past." [everyone is on the path whether they realize it or not; there is no room for guilt or shame, only mindfulness and readiness to pick up the journey and Goal once again].

- "I am now a teacher, not a student." [the best guides and teachers always continue seeking knowledge and wisdom themselves].

7. Surrender, Remove Subtle Ego, Be Humble, and Receive with Gratitude

- Surrender means attunement. One merges personal will with Supreme will. One merges with the Supreme like an individual wave rejoins the vast ocean.
- The seeker can eliminate all hindrances through humility, enthusiasm, patience, and perseverance.
- The wise seeker finds that the entire universe is available to assist along the path to Supreme Consciousness ["knock and the doors will open, ask and ye shall receive"].
- The first step on the spiritual journey is to wake up and recognize that the true Goal of life is not "out there" but rather "in here." [pretending to be awake will simply leave one asleep].
- One can convert even mundane activities and objectives into steps toward Self within.
- Life naturally will provide external lessons, challenges, and opportunities.
- An experienced traveler on the path can provide invaluable assistance to those willing to learn
- A legitimate guide can assist the seeker to find lasting inner peace and contentment irrespec-

tive of internal conditions or eternal challenges.
• All the doors are open.

8. Key Elements of the Spiritual Path

Spiritual Discernment (Vivek)

Spiritual discernment allows one to recognize impermanent and permanent, real and illusive. truth
and untruth. The pandemic and other disasters
remind us of the impermanent nature of life. One
sees that all things change and also an underlying
presence of love in all things and people.

When we look around, we observe and witness all
kinds of changes. If we remain centered and
aware, this exercise brings us closer to permanent
Self. The pandemic is a largely unknown process
that is impacting human society. It is not to be
feared, but rather used to heighten awareness of
external fragility and to build internal strength
among all.

Renunciation (Vairagya)

By experiencing impermanence directly, one naturally cultivates renunciation. One learns to live in
the present without holding onto anyone or anything. Renunciation means that attraction to the
world disappears naturally as one comes closer to

the Self. One becomes introverted without the distractions of worldly desire.

Liberation (Mumuksha)

One wakes up to realize the true goal of life and the futility of pursuing wordly goals. One increases desire for true freedom and becomes established on the spiritual path. This deep desire becomes the undercurrent that regulates all activities of life.

Swadhyay

Swadhyay means Self-inquiry and contemplation of the original scriptures. This is one of the five niyamas or steps to inner purification described in Patanjali's Raja Yoga. One will benefit through regular practice.

Satsang

Satsang means discussion of truth and association with other evolved souls. This provides inspiration and guidance needed to sustain enthusiasm and progress on the spiritual path. Satsang is particularly helpful during times of external distraction and large-scale challenges such as the present-day pandemic, economic recession, social division, and other problems that are part of the present age.

Perseverance

Perseverance means continuous effort and adhering to the path toward God or Self in spite of difficulties, successes, and failure. All obstacles should be met with a smiling face and enthusiasm. One can see the pandemic as a period during which there is more time available to devote to persistent attention to the Source of all life.

Patience

Patience means sustaining steadiness as one anticipates positive change. This is a critically importance aspect of the spiritual path and a form of austerity (Tapas). One remains steady in mind and heart during periods of anticipation, success, and failure. One remembers and practices the love and patience of one's parents and that of God.

Affirmations

- I accept myself.
- I love myself.
- I love life and the creation of God.
- All beings are created in the image of God and have divinity within them.
- All living creatures are interconnected.
- All living creatures are my family members
- I expand my consciousness and pray for the well-being of all living creatures.
- I thank God for all the gifts of life.

- I accept these gifts as privileges.
- God is my mother, father, brother, companion, my wealth and knowledge.
- Whatever I do with my thoughts, speech and actions, I offer to the Lord.
- I am an instrument of God and serve creation unconditionally.
- I am surrounded by love and share my love with everyone.
- I am content here and now. I am surrounded by God's grace.
- I do not need to go anywhere or do anything.

Ancient Sanskrit Prayer

Dear Lord,

Lead me from untruth to truth (Untruth is changing material universe and truth is the eternal supreme consciousness)

Lead me from darkness to light (Darkness is ignorance of Maya and light is the spark of divine consciousness).

Lead me from mortality to immortality (Mortality is the transmigration of jivatma or soul and immortality is liberation)

May all living creatures remain healthy and happy. May everyone find good fortune and no one suffer.

The Quantum Leap

The recognition that life is short and uncertain leads to a sense of urgency. One seeks truth with urgency when life is ending or full of uncertainty as during the pandemic. The answers rest with the Self within. We can access Self quickly with focused energy and urgent effort.

- Quantum leap is a sudden awakening that transforms life, just like an electron jumps an orbit.
- Quantum leap takes place when one is shocked into awakening with a death in the family, a terminal disease, or other major life challenges.
- Quantum leap means to be willing to sacrifice ego in order to be transformed, just like a seed it destroyed and becomes a fruitful plant.
- Quantum leap is the result of accumulated and properly channeled energy. Just as steam is accumulated and made to run an engine, we can accumulate energy and quickly direct it toward awareness of Self or God.
- One needs clarity of intention, intensity, urgency, undercurrent of goal and visualization for making a quantum leap.
- One needs urgency like your house is on fire. Even a paralyzed person can gain a temporary burst of energy to save his or her life. One does not need instructions with such urgency.

You can bypass all the rituals and means and can go directly to destination, which is the Self (Atman). Let go of all beliefs and conditioning. You do not need any effort but can simply realize your essential nature (Bliss). It is similar to taking an elevator to reach higher floors bypassing the steps.

Quantum Leap Meditation

The spiritual heart center is located within the chest cavity where you feel your true being (Atman). Supreme Consciousness dwells within the heart as Atman and has the qualities of eternal existence (Sat) and consciousness (Chit) of the bliss experience (Anand). Atman is our eternal nature and present at all times. We have forgotten it due to ignorance (Avidya) and cosmic illusion (Maya).

Feel the roots of your being in the heart center. I-Consciousness is the trunk. Mind, senses, and body are the branches, leaves, flowers, and fruits.

Be quiet and ask the question: "Who am I?" Dive within effortlessly to reach the source of your being. Self (Atman) constantly pulls living creatures (Jivatma).

We can experience it directly when we relax and becomes free from the grip of material attractions (Maya).

<u>Guidance:</u>

- Withdraw your awareness from the body, senses, and the mind.
- Remain focused on the heart center.
- This is the eternal center of bliss untouched by the turmoil of the impermanent material universe.
- Remain focused and experience peace and contentment.
- Let the experience saturate your body, senses, and mind (gross, astral, and causal bodies).
- Let the experience expand to all leaving creatures until you become homogeneous with all.
- Dualities dissolve. You experience your being within and without (transcend space and time).
- This is the quantum leap. You do not need any secret steps or sophisticated effort.
- Retain the experience as long as desired.
- It can be recalled during the active day.
- Awareness of Atman remains in the background while performing all activities.
- It will provide intuition and guidance and deep peace in life.
- Practice this meditation before going to sleep.

A Practical Opportunity for Today

The spiritual path is the most efficient means for finding lasting happiness and success in life. The spiritual path naturally fosters love for Self and others. When we tune into our own nature, love flows. This produces both energy and proper perspective on life. Life ultimately directs everyone to God or Self. Whether this understanding comes near the beginning, middle, or end of life; during challenging times, peaceful times, or times of strife; the path cannot be avoided. Thus, it is wise to maintain a continual focus on the real Goal of life (Self-Realization) and enjoy the journey no matter the view.

Four basic principles are recommended for those wishing to advancing quickly on the spiritual path: (1) Prioritizing one's spiritual goals, (2) Persevering in the search for God or Self with Patience, and (3) Surrendering to the Supreme being and to the results of one's quest for spiritual knowledge.

Most seekers today use the spiritual path for subtle entertainment, to find immediate relief, to justify escape from duties, or to fulfill spiritual fantasies. Many remain attached to their own beliefs and defend these instead of searching for truth within. Life goes on with the illusion of being spiritual. One finds followers to support a given ideology and forgets about the original search for God. This leaves everyone asleep. One does not become a critic of his or her own behavior. One does not evaluate self-progress.

In truth, the subtle experience of God or Self occurs only within. The spiritual path involves a humble and continual search within. The real path is lonely and best suited for the wise and the brave.

Because the Goal is infinitely rewarding, there is no reason to stop treading the path even if you begin to experience peace. A knowledgeable guide can offer guidance to speed the traveler along the journey to consciousness of God or bliss. A spiritually thirsty person welcomes such assistance, but ultimately travels the path alone.

We are passing through a period of spiritual darkness (Kali yuga) during which immorality, injustice and untruth are on the rise. We are distracted with technology and an overload of information. We are losing the capacity to think for ourselves and choose the direction that is best for our own being.

Contact Yogi Shanti Desai

The present public health challenges lead us back to ourselves. The only real control we have of the pandemic is to recognize the importance of our own being and that of others. This leads us to wear masks, maintain distance between each other, have patience, and embrace the opportunity to slow down and experience Self or God within.

The current pandemic has presented humanity with new challenges and difficulties. Such challenges have existed throughout human history. The difference today is failing leadership and widespread changes in ethics and morality.

The seeker should keep in mind that periods of rapid change and destruction always lead to new life. Perhaps the most positive change in the present era is the availability of technology that can be used to bring or refresh wisdom and guidance for use by the spiritual seeker. Ancient scriptures and spiritual guides that may have taken years to access can now be reached in an instant.

Today, yoga lessons and spiritual guidance can be accessed without even leaving one's home. For this reason, and with the intent of providing experience and knowledge to those who are sincerely interested, Yogi Shanti Desai is offering short weekly Yoga Zoom Meetings or longer Yoga Zoom Meetings on a monthly basis. Based on individual and group interest, spiritual guidance programs can be designed to meet practical and financial needs during the pandemic.

The meetings are forms of Swadhyay and Satsang, both of which are vitally useful to both new and well-traveled seekers and yoga practitioners.

This is an ideal time in history to wake up and embrace or renew the path to Self and truth. Come join us.

Yogi Shanti Desai

Email: yogishantidesai@cs.com
Website: www.yogishantidesai.com
Phone: 609-380-7944

Publications by Yogi Shanti Desai

Yoga: Holistic Practice Manual	1976
Hatha Yoga Practice Manual	1978
Meditation Practice Manual	1981
Reality Here and Now	1996
Self- I, Me, Mine, Ours, Illusions	2002
Dynamic Balanced Living	2004
Dynamic Meditation for Living	2006
Dynamic Quantum Transformation	2007
Personal to Global Transformation	2007
Wisdom for Living	2009
The Secret of Bliss	2011
Dynamic Spiritual Transformation	2012
Zero is Infinity	2015
Wake Up- Reflections for Spiritual Awakening	2017
Quantum Leap to Liberation	2017
Spiritual Awakening in the Age of Kali Yuga	2018
Threefold Path to Bliss	2018
Transformation of Consciousness	2020
Eternal Reality	2020

About the Co-Author

Edward Glazier, PhD is a career anthropologist with an ongoing interest in human interaction with the natural world. His professional interests are scientific in nature and his spiritual interests stem from the facts that organized religion offers little to those seeking Truth here and now. Ed met Yogi Desai in 1981 and continues to be deeply inspired by his teachings nearly 40 years later.

9 798567 790267